Against Paradise

BOOKS BY SHAWNA LEMAY

All the God-Sized Fruit (1999)
Against Paradise (2001)

Against Paradise

Poems by

Shawna Lemay

M&S

Canadian Cataloguing in Publication Data

Lemay, Shawna, 1966–
Against paradise

ISBN 0-7710-5227-8

I. Title.

PS8573.E5358A73 2001   C811'.54   C00-932930-7
PR9199.3.L45A73 2001

We acknowledge the financial support of the Government of
Canada through the Book Publishing Industry Development Program
for our publishing activities. We further acknowledge the support of the
Canada Council for the Arts and the Ontario Arts Council for our
publishing program.

Typeset in Garamond by M&S, Toronto
Printed and bound in Canada

McClelland & Stewart Ltd.
The Canadian Publishers
481 University Avenue
Toronto, Ontario
M5G 2E9
www.mcclelland.com

1 2 3 4 5   05 04 03 02 01

For Rob and Chloe

CONTENTS

I

THE SLIMNESS OF REALITY

MY VENICE

I have brought you here for
this.

Plunked you into this gawdawful charming armchair.
I've been suspended there, too
smelling the bowls of dust sunk into plush upholstery.
Traced my fingers along the threadbare crimson velvet arms
pictured my body disposed
below the surface of slow running water.

I've not brought you here
to sink a stiletto into your breast
or trim off your head with a hatchet.

Behold the Venetian dagger.

Compact, elegant.
Subtly tinted blade of Murano glass
encased in polished metal.
The glass breaks at the haft
with a gentle thrust
into the victim's belly.
Guaranteed to leave a wound
that has the victim say,
indeed 'tis nothing, the merest scratch, a nick.
Comes in mauve, periwinkle, garnet, and chartreuse.
Scrollwork optional.
Festering begins immediately.

The Damned Rapturous Beauty of Things

Here, everything has been said.

And so liberated from words
mouths open
echo
sound ripples.
Old lies are told.
Gelatinous ones
snow-white lies, lies of omission
blatant lies, lies spoken through yellow uneven teeth.
Fastidious, impeccably dressed, dark lies.
Calculated lies, the colour of bruised plums.
Dirty, ochre lies of necessity.
Devious lies, treacherous ones
the fussy blue of sky abandoning raindrops like sewing needles.
Diaphanous ones told in a moment of passion.
Watery lies of complicity, evasion, desperation.
Tawdry, decrepit little lies.
Lies about the damned rapturous beauty of things.

Holy untruths
carried through air the scent
of recycled vermouth
rotten eggs.
Over water
aphid green and sepia
lime Jell-O
sap.

Here, lies are uttered with the solemn wit of buoyed stones.
Here, lies are loose and easy
obsessive.

If I said
there is a colour here
nameless
revolutionary.
Source of all irrational truth.
Reflected in water
its source unknowable.

You would believe this.
Would you?

RECLINING ON VELVET

A glamorous tragedy.
And then
ashes scattered
in an orchard of pomegranates
when leaves are golden
and the swallows gone quiet.
Ever after
people would revisit my last words.
Something snappier than Browning's
"how gratifying."
Or
I would lie down in a classical garden
having chewed on violet petals
until my lips were purple
heaving in rapacious air
cursing the twisted aesthetics of gardens
until no more was I.

That's how I once pictured my demise.

Now, I know I'll have to take up chain-smoking
drink quarts of apricot liqueur.
I'll move to Venice
die there
as Robert Browing did.
Wait for my last words.
And hope for
suddenly.

Make arrangements to have my remains
disguised as
holy knick-knacks.
I'll design reliquaries of gilt and smoked glass
lined with plush crimson.
Wrist bone, fifth rib, index finger.
Lock of hair. Vial of blood.
When I'm gone
it would be nice to know
my bloodless, withered, impatient heart
was reclining on velvet
below a stone
set amongst the tesserae of a floor mosaic
in a city
that always laughed at poetry.

Papier Offerings

Once upon a
time
there lived a princess
in an illusory palazzo
surrounded by water the colour of saffron and lapis lazuli.
The rooms were full of feckless furniture
Louis XIV
false fainting sofas
sham tables and chairs
bogus bureaus
mendacious chandeliers.

All but the bed
papier mâché.
A real bed infinitely more comfortable, dreamable
than one made of the sour outpouring
of daily news and bleached flour.

She had meant to go on and papier mâché
furniture for the poor, the downtrodden
couldn't get a soul
to accept these
offerings
no matter
how energetically she described
the symbolism.

What the Pigeon Muttered, Piazza San Marco

A party of unruffled pigeons
methodically desperate
are we,
quoth she.

The relatives are distinguished, medalled.
Illustrious. Non-denominational. Task-oriented.

No disrespect
I prefer
common
desultory
pagan.

Day
examine the fabric of a city's detritus
sun-dried gelato, waffle-cone crumb
cigarette butt with cotton candy smudge
wrapper, pebble – shiny.
Never stop moving
no   stop
moving silent
head cocked.

Hand with bread.
Popular trick, alight on arm
flapflapflap
the stately departure in unison
photograph
theatrics

return to earth
as though there were a message.

The secrets I might hold in these gnarled claws.
Memories of shattered mirrors
like wilted poems.

Hand with bread.
I romance stone ears
translating old mysteries.

Night
rest in the terror under bridges
coocoocoo.
I perch in the frangible ecstasy
of shadow and delight
in the savage quivering.

In Delirium ad Infinitum

Venice. Pale, damp-plumed, glittering dream
remain distant and aloof

because I,
inebriated by future cities
golden
will allow you to capsize
forget you are real.

Would you have me yearn and lean
towards you
until I am a bitter, crooked woman?
Restless
in delirium ad infinitum
indolently jealous
of intrepid travellers.

I stay home.
I stay home.

This drab and fickle
delectable living we do.

DETAIL OF SANDAL

When someone speaks about Venice
a little bit is shaved off
then taken up by wind or water
or lands on someone's shoe
which gets thrown in a suitcase, carried away.

And if I were to have you imagine
our honeymoon
nights at the Hotel Brooklyn
supremely lazy mornings
cups of coffee
lemonade taken under bridges
sun ravishing
blonde hair white
too white flesh
pink
everything delightful
indelible erasable memories
cool churches
red drapery
small faithful dogs
museums full of Madonnas.

Imagine this, detail of sandal:
thin leather sole
between me and terra not so firma.
Later, it would require clever fixing
a hairpin
on a long road in Sardinia

but in Venice
it held.

If I were to tell you anything else
I fear
love romance marriage childbirth
might vanish.
I fear
being responsible for an eighth of an inch of stone
shearing off with questionable grace into the great slough.

I've just now returned from the wardrobe
sandal absent, a hairpin languors on the tile.

The Slimness of Reality

Under a small, jeering strip of sapphire sky,
a slender blue scarf
even now
in the slimness of reality
someone devises this baroque ruse
mad plan, diaphanous dream, graceful fantasy
designs invitations, crushed velvet words.
You are cordially invited to the three tenors concert
in Piazza San Marco.

Once there, the throngs wait
in tuxedoes and sequin mermaid gowns
wait for the sun to set
breathe the sewage-moist air.

Afterwards, they remember
calm shuffling in the half-light
that unrecoverable glow.
Waiting amongst shameless steel-grey pigeons
while the café bands duel.

They wait
for the red velvet curtain to be released from its moorings.
It collapses
with a puff of dust into a grimy crimson puddle

And there it is
this arcane, impossible, enigmatical colour leaks into air
contains all the loss and violence and despair
and love and pleasure in the world and in a blaze –

a glimpse of the intricate architecture of things and
the dirt and the decrepit symbolism
and the astonishing ravishing
simple glamourless complicated
truth.

The moment before
a rhapsody of second-rate, derivative fabrication.
The next moment
pink champagne intoxication
the cruel charity of fresh fallen snow
the scent of earth and dew-laden rose petals
implausible
fleeting
doomed.

II

MASQUERADE

Story of a Teacup

To tell this story of a teacup properly
I would need a year of perfume, clouds and solitude
immersion in the world's literature
and a knowledge of things of which I know not.

I have things to say to myself, however
and to you, too.
I would devise cities if it were necessary.

If I knew more, perhaps I would begin with
what I was wearing that day,
my name, George Sand,
a comment on the nature of love, passion,
or something about Alfred's illness, his mad raving
undraped romping, his
indiscretions.
How we were both stricken
with dysentery upon arriving in Venice.
Risible.
There'd be a bit about the doctor.
How I poured out words to fulfill contracts, to pay bills
while he gave and gave.
How together we nursed my abandoned delirious lover.

It's a fact that teacups figure in many stories.
Some with flowers on them
some with fine patterns in blue and gold.
They are dainty things
capable of holding scalding liquid
that much is true.

If I were another woman I might tell you
what this particular teacup featured.
I haven't time to be anyone other than myself
in any number of disguises.

Others would begin with arrivals
romance
miraculous sunrise from some point on the water
or departures
heartsick
return to some other more real life.

For Alfred, this single teacup meant
that the doctor and myself had placed lips
on a shared surface
revealing intimacies, deceit, frailty.

Where there's a drained teacup balanced near the edge
of some table, chairs pushed back
whether by a window overlooking the Grand Canal
or some other body of water
or even a field, an orchard or a row of houses
I must insist there's a story.
By all means, tell it.
At the risk of fouling the entire.

A TRIO FOR LADY MARY WORTLEY MONTAGU

I. A Woman, Packing (July 1739)

Not sewing, lace-making, or cooking
not writing or reading
or gazing out a window at hedgerows and geese
not doing laundry or scrubbing anything
not reclining, bathing

but packing.
Thirteen lucky trunks.
Destined
to reside in dark gardens of fire.

So much to take, so much to leave behind.

I am off to find you wrote Lady Mary to Francesco Algarotti
also known as the Swan of Padua.

Her passion speaks and therefore
words, mere needles and coloured thread
piercing cloth, wearing eyes blind –
embroidered things,
unnecessary.

In the inventory of items taken:
needlework, of course
some complete, some in progress.
No doubt, scenes of domestic bliss
long unravelled
and then, the one of a goddess chasing a golden swan.

As for the rest
let's, for the sake of simplicity, say
her trunks were full
of feathers
one for each pang of longing
each disappointment, betrayal,
each treacle of treachery
each couplet of gossip.

This is when the drab deceptions begin in earnest.
This is when keys are placed in locks and turned.
This is when the weight of things is measured.

Day before departure
there is a total eclipse of the sun lasting one hour
and if there were anyone recording her facial expressions
which there wasn't
would they have found her
eyes limpid pools, smouldering orbs, or confused constellations?

II. In the Desert without Mirrors

At a party of gods and goddesses
a bowl is dropped, broken.
A candy dish perhaps.
A trifle?
The result is a city – Venice.

Paradise, you discovered,
was made of splintered bits of coloured glass
well lit.

Once, you flew to the sun, radiant, enthralled
were eclipsed
landed on your feet here.
And so after years in exile
the place would call.
You would answer.

This time though,
you are older, nearly seventy.
You attend opera only if masks are to be worn
because you are mortified by wrinkles.
You have forsaken mirrors
marked by the pox now
longer than not.
But there is music again.

There is music
when you walk, robed, barefoot, in the piazza.
When you are elbow to elbow with throngs of grand tourists
it is as though
you are in the desert without mirrors
solitary as a grain of sand.

III. By Way of Glass

Fool, you left.

You had your reasons.
(See footnote or
wait for the movie.)

Besides which
there were cancerous cells
invading your body.
Your journey home through wars.
But arriving, the most disquieting.

Home, the oddest place of all.
And you its nuovo curio.
Lion with a ball balanced on its nose.
Come one, come all, come see.

The country of your first breath
embalms.

You wish for the civility of masks.
All these matters to attend to
everyone pretending to know you
the refuge of inkwells too slender
where it held mountains and monuments.
Once even the moon
from the vantage of an arbour.

You begin your sojourn to stone
(through the labyrinth of rumours
through the dusty hall of mirrors)

by way of glass.
Shattered.
By way of
foolish craving
for that candy-dish city.

You died a profoundly
undocumented death
with nary a thought for future biographers
rifling poets
who must leave you in a foggy, obvious country
in a damp bed
gesturing with longing towards a city
that would have at least fabricated
the end.

Through the Stained Glass Window All of Us Damp Birds

The night after, I dreamed
I'd delved into his chest cavity
plucked Shelley's heart from blackness and embers
slumped it into my carpet bag.
Then, William such a little boy
found me a pail of clay
together we made her up again, my Clara Everina
with coloured glass for eyes and shards for soft hair
plump, the most beautiful creature
her smile a perfect pink rose
dressed her in white leather boots
lace-trimmed dress, bonnet.
Then we loved her enough
alive
jumped through the stained glass window all of us damp birds
into a gondola and left
her acquaintance with the sinking city one hour.

The next day was a submersion in ice and water.
I, the last woman
that alone.
Wasted for the pleasures of hate.
Even that.

I should have gone mad
the way dreams and fiction and living
tangled and twisted
one lost in the other
advance retreat spin in a circle

let me go
blindfolded
my hands on fire
Mary, Mary so bloody-damned contrary
and no one notices
she had a little lamb
the lamb no more.
And I.

Mrs. Radcliffe
were your dreams beautiful
and sublime?
Cliffhangers.
You'd wake at the end of a chapter.
Wait until next slumber to find yourself
lost again
O the terror
O the horror
in that dream maze
where everything glows
saffron and throbs melancholy purple.
And the line between pulchritude
and monstrosity
is indeed fine and insubstantial.

Never having been there
did you dream Venice?
You read Hester Thrale Piozzi's
Observations and Reflections, etc.
late at night by candlelight
under a heavy, heavy quilt.
Morning.
The forgotten colours of dreaming
become a carnival of scents
parade of perfume.
You write
travelling behind the pictures of dreams
speechless

come up through the water of dreams
breathing.

You write of that lost place
forgotten place
where you lived a forgotten faraway life.
Drank cappuccino, elegantly, before cappuccino was drunk.

Mrs. Radcliffe
were you lost in your sweet diluted dreams
and did you find your way
float your way
home?

THE FEMALE CASANOVA

"Cleopatra's nose, had it been shorter, the whole face of the world would have been changed." – Blaise Pascal, *Pensées*

Speaking of confessions.
I rather think of Peggy Guggenheim more
as a foiled Cleopatra
than the female Casanova.

Before she came to collect art
before addiction
bored
she went for a nose job
abandoned under a local
because the doctor couldn't perform
a Tennysonian "tip-tilted like a flower" manoeuvre.

I rather imagine
she was lonely, love-starved
afraid of being caught
beneath love's tawdry disguises
forlorn clown, ragged beggar, feather boa flapper.
Bright glass, vain, imprisoned in a wire gate.

Afraid that someone would discover her life was fantasy
comedy even
and then she would slip
into a rotten reality
with no palaces, rooftop gardens, beloved Lhasa Apsos.
And after the slip
her throne would sink into fractured air

she would be heiress to a copper penny
no bona fide eccentric
no Mark Antony
would ever sign her guest book.

But what do I know of changing
the unfathomable course of history?
And what do I know of hunger and fear?
And what do I know of the chandelier heart?
Peering into this burning
library of stone
its catalogue of chimera.

Painting the Garden Lilac at the Nonfinito

*"Now I'm going to speak of the sadness of flowers in order to feel
more fully the order of what exists."*
– Clarice Lispector, *The Stream of Life*

Forget that she tangoed with leopards
while the nude pianist tickled
the ivories.
Here was a woman who refused
the sadness of flowers.

Forget the servants
wearing gold spray paint
holding trays of canapés and grapes
and fizzling cocktails.
Forget the apes and the Afghans roaming.

She threw parties, Marchesa Luisa Casati did
at the Nonfinito
the topless Palazzo Venier dei Leoni.
There were no tame lions
heads like ripe sunflowers
as there once were.
This was no museum
as it would become when Peggy Guggenheim left it.
Here, there is no Angel of the Citadel.

In a garden which ought not to have existed
raised above slough and surrounded by stone
that which does not exist
requests pondering.
Not pondering.

Remember. Everything in the garden lilac.
Stones, benches, grass, potted plants, trees, walkways.
Lilac-coloured roses, geraniums, daisies.
Fresh.
The painter bypasses the canvas
goes directly to life
stills life, lilac,
time.

Morning and the revellers are drenched
drowning
in the perfume of what isn't.

Tangled and Insignificant

It was June.
He was twenty years younger than George, Mary Ann.
Their honeymoon.
Mrs. Cross, now.

*

*I am the criminal usually known under the name
George Eliot.*

*

It was a temporary illness brought on by
excess heat
foul air
and the illusory and insubstantial time spent
intangibly bobbling about
in a shady black black gondola.

*

Henry James called her
magnificently ugly – deliciously hideous.

*

The other George, George Lewes.
All those years and years
they lived in sin
he loved her delicate, swamp-coloured eyes.
Once
they were together in fairyland
they looked out the window of a cheap hotel
and saw the sunbeams empty of dust

the way it must be in heaven.
Their days were tangled and ripe
with insignificance.

*

Once two humans are bound
the gauzy threads of their lives
become tangled.
They wear those knots around their necks
like lost jewellery
for always.

*

John Cross walked into their upscale hotel room
that afternoon.
The masks she'd ordered had arrived and George
was sitting in the window seat
wearing hers.
It was to be a surprise
a joke.

Horse heads.
Palomino and Piebald.
Blast Henry James.
She could laugh at herself.
Until she cried.
The tears soaking the papier mâché
soggy.

*

What would it mean in a story
if an ugly woman were to be loved
by a handsome man?

*

Cross walked into the room
cursing
dreading hoping
for the absurd solemnity
of a literary love scene.

Moon dust everywhere
the air filled with the stuff
as he catapulted through the pane glass
landing in that pungent broth, the Grand Canal.
His hair streaked with algae
dripping and stinking
they fished him out
flailing.

*

George Eliot died six months later.
John Cross lived until he was eighty-four.

Thru All the Afternoon Till Dark

"These last few days I have been sitting to Millais from immedi-
ately after breakfast to dinner, thru all the afternoon till dark."
– Effie Ruskin, *Effie in Venice*

I've been holding this pose, effortless
irretrievable.
Which is capital.
The painting is to be named *The Order of Release*.
I'm daydreaming, naturally,
in the way that thoughts become muddled
serious nonsense.
I begin to imagine myself
one of Millais' Ophelias
the glazed foliage and flowers, the romantic picky details
passing me by
and then I'm floating down the Grand Canal
with primrose in my hair and then seaweed
sticks and froth.
But then, no, I drop that thread
begin to remember those hide-and-seek days
before John and I moved to this ugly house with the quaint yard.
Don't mind what I've said elsewhere
at this moment I can say in all honesty
I've not been happy, not with him, no, not ever.
There were letters home
I described the brittle bones of the city he deciphered,
sketched, caressed,
and shocked taking daguerreotypes.
I described navigating the labyrinth, fluid,
piloting my own water-coffin

all the admiring gazes
pink dresses, besmirched
paintings of Madonnas.
I was ill, off, and spoke cheerfully of leeches
and hair-gloves, stroking my body, solitary and demure.
Oh, letters from abroad are always the worst packet of filthy fibs.
Dry, flowery fibs squashed between sepia descriptions
of things great, grand, and altogether foreign.
Of things steeped in an unfathomable fierce history.
Our six-year marriage, unconsummated.
I was lost in a tangle of half-shells and seafoam
fresh roses, crumbling stones, footbridges, boats and masks.
I was lost, bound.
And now lost in thought all afternoon, tranquil
I see it is dark again.
While he paints, Millais waxes on the quality of my wrist bones
ravishes metatarsus
speaks of the painfully exquisite
rendering he could accomplish of my left elbow.
Whatever else, these words are
the order for my release.

In Which Fictional Character Speaks to Deceased Author, or Renata to Mr. Hemingway

Kind sir, I am willing
to exist some kind of male fantasy
ink girl, weak black watery lines
decorated with so much seafoam.

Neither do I regret my depiction
as a portrait within your novel.
It is fine that you have me wrapped and tied near the end
a brown parcel first in a tin-can boat
then in the back seat of a Buick
when you escape from our city, my city.

I'm glad to have sipped so many truly dry martinis at Harry's.
To have been born a Venetian.
I am by the way forgiving
of the true lady after whom I am modelled
and who said how dull and un-Venetian she found me.

I do not mind truly I am so very repetitious
and altogether too beautiful and young and long-haired
concerned with the shape of my mouth
and unbelievably indifferent to my true and simple beauty
and above the artifice of other women
and I quite forgive the infamous gondola scene
and I quite forgive Dante and Beatrice.
And it's fine that I weep in the end
since it is true I am made from liquid.
And it's fine because I do not neglect your blood, sweat, or tears.

I am only sorry, kind sir,
that water will sometimes turn to ice
that the heart of one so young as I
is a stone palace in love with its glittering reflection.
That my heart is the dream
of a wanderer in search of a peeled orange
on an open palm
or a species of water lily invented around a fire in winter.

But it's true in the end
though you may find this rough
I exist and so
easily I swim off the page.
Yours truly.

To Bask in Amnesiac Splendour

What do I care about the intricacies of flattery
these ancient wild days
these days that hum golden and burn blue
these blind exotic days.

Yes, I am blind and old in this insoluble city like Babylonian lace
left to bask in amnesiac splendour.
No one remembers anything about being
here.

That was my secret and I haven't told you.

The guidebook or bearleader must have told all the young lads
you have Rosalba Carriera take your likeness in pastel.
Praise the cubs for originality
I've made a decent living and kept my hands relatively clean.

Don't hold it against me –
every portraitist flatters a paying sitter
don't believe otherwise.
And there's no other picture needs
its buyer so much, so carefully.

So I captured pure desire
made it look like nonchalance.
Uneasiness and foolish bewilderment
translated, cheated
into
comfortable arrogance.

Omit confusion, trepidation, frustration
omit disillusionment, distrust
omit fatigue, unease
omit homesick
omit constipation
omit heightened awareness of mortality
omit feelings of inadequacy
omit fear of the unknown.

They packed
to take home
an enchanted confident jaunty
pristine
mask.

My sacrifice, their elegant electric vision.

Useless Opalescent Wings

Who am I? Who am I?
asks the dramatic monologue.
Call me Failure, Chimera
call me names.
I've heard the insults, the sniggering.
Who am I?

Waxen-winged cherub
I was born too close to their flame.
Offspring of beautiful genius
I was doomed to grow scales, claws, useless
opalescent wings.
Where they kindled some sacred flame
I breathed indiscriminate repugnant fire.
I wore precious jewels, gaudy and they were
scandalous, foul because I wore them.
Who am I?

Misshapen sonnet.
Married for money, not love.
How do I love thee let me count
and count the ways.
Who am I?

When your dreams are lost to you at birth
you go to find them where you know you can't.
Venice, my erotic scintillating dream.
Dreamer in the dream is desirable
is human after all.

I awake
to mythic dissatisfaction.

I pretend to become an artist.
Is it impossible to hope that a man of no talent or taste
could paint one masterpiece?
Repulsive, loathsome, unholy thing – but
about it something pure, transcendent?
Something desperately heartbreaking, breathtaking?

I know I am not the misunderstood genius
but my canvases get bigger and bigger
so many expectations to paint over
and that awful Christmas card child with ringlets
and apple cheeks.

I am Pen, son of
Elizabeth Barrett and Robert Browning.

But, forgive me, I digress.
Who am I?

AGAINST PARADISE
(Poems for Alice Monet)

Expulsion of Bees

We left Giverny that autumn
grieving bumbling
and stupid with honey
no, let's not go
we said.

Flowers, always, evermore
Monet said.

His bewildering heart required huge meals,
many courses.
But he was seduced
by an infinity of flowers.

It was our paradise in progress, Giverny
fine muddle
undisciplined green, boiling with vagrant blooms.
Yet what a relief to escape it was.
Human again, mortal
and how.
Enough of the interminable gloomy water lilies, Monet, enough.
I was, then, against paradise.

We departed timorous as bees
to the land of multifarious lions
wild with imagining.

Arrived October One, 1908.

Quarrel with Light

The trip begins with
refusal
to touch his brushes.
I chew nails, discreetly wring my hard hands.
Stupid beauty, idiot painter, paint, paint, I think.

The empty canvases arrive, he goes out into the plain air.
Drinks of it.
Tastes.
Full, he paints.
I breathe again.

He becomes a seaborne confectioner
instigates a reckless
clotted quarrel with light
attacks the canvas with a demented rain of daubs
vicious kisses
never tempted to look over his shoulder with mirrors.

I watch, lulled
by the sea, the sea, the sea.

We are always leaving tomorrow.

Glass and Glitz

Monet and I in the piazza posing.
Pigeons everywhere.
One on his head.

This is ridiculous, but all right then
I thought. Why not.

We'd been agog inside St. Mark's.
Garden turned to glass and glitz
some ancient spell.
Appealed to Monet's sense of horror
vacui.

He wanted some zealous god to pick it up and shake it
send the fog in
paint the guts of it that way.

I only wanted to kiss the walls
awaken it so.

This Dark Lemon Leaving

We will return, we whispered
as all who abandon do.

Silly, replies the city.
I care not, replies Venice.

I cannot stand
this dark lemon leaving.

It was not so perfect
and sweet as I would have liked.

Leave-taking never is.

O, Barbarous Moonlight

You will think that, when I'm gone, soon gone.
You see
I know you so well, Monet.

And then, you'll wonder
what jams there'll be for breakfast.
No matter, that's why I loved you.

Before bed you'll talk to a photograph of me
beside a saucer of miscellaneous flower petals.
You'll ask my image what is the point of paint
the mucky chaos of colour
and why why why.

Just paint.
Just paint.

I have no answers for you, funny passionate old man.
Paint your hazy candy-coloured Venice
before it vanishes in your mind.
Paint your knots and tangles and rat's nests and be done with it.
Like always.
As ever.

Poor dear thing.

The moonlight more like béchamel.

III

FREE OF THE TRAGEDY OF WORDS

The Inferior Realms

I hadn't thought to remove
my sandals
until years later and oceans apart
seeing the plan of the pavement
San Marco, drawn by Antonio Visentini.

I wasn't drawn to the down-below of it all
to the inferior realms
I wasn't pulled to the grit and murk
or to the pattern and design.
Distracted by the beauty of overkill
I was all eyes and
maybe it was nearly lunch
and I wanted a shrimp sandwich, wine.
Maybe I was tired and wanted to hear the water
and sit and drift and daydream a little.

Some say you can never really go back home.
The same goes for vacations.

Some believe that paradise is not lost.
It's under our noses.
I can tell you now I neglected
the thick, battered soles of my feet.

It may have been there.
Step on the right combination and wham
you've got stars in your mouth
you're spirographically drowning
the stone seeds awake and sprout

the rock carpet lifts you up, graceful.
That's why they never let dogs in the church.
They know
it's just that easy.

JUDITH *II*, GALLERIA D'ARTE MODERNA, VENICE

Judith II, promise
escape

you are clearly poised and positioned

lay down
decapitation, masks
shed press-on nails
gnaw bracelets

skirt design
and flee, femme fatale
slough that cryptic cryogenic gold
slither
drag that magic carpet.

In your dangerous inebriation
elimination
dance
give birth.

I will meet you
in San Marco
at midnight
and we shall seek asylum
camouflaged
by coloured rocks, alone
and wait for the stray ship of thoughts
and wait by the tumultuous sea, all serenity.

Capriccio:

painter's vacation.

Every voyage is a voyage home.
Further towards making some imaginary upside-down sense
of whence you came and however
did your heart become so stained
and mixed upon like a glass palette
and you've always been half in love with being lost
with discovery, disappearing or running away
with the sea's commotion, or with the banter of stone.
You've loved certain cities originally and lopsidedly
you've turned over leaves in certain cities and you're the sort who
lives in dreams like caves
for the sake of certain cities.

There are scenes of Venice
the furniture rearranged, redone.
Attempting to make a departure in paint
to invent future worlds,
the painter arrives home.

What I'm trying to say is, don't fall in love
with anything I may or may not have said.
If I sent you postcards they were merely
elaborations on the horror
of finding dreams insufficient
and reality implausible.
If I painted you a picture
it was wet and you
in your finery and plumes, pressed against it.

WHOSE NAME IS FLUID

Is it fair?

Bellini has one named after him.
Champagne with a splash of peach juice.
Titian, too. The Tiziano! Exclamation point optional.
Champagne, grape and pomegranate juice.

The Bellini glows, triple-glaze sunrise
tickles and slinks all the way down your esophagus.
The Tiziano – you want to dip your pinky
drink the whole thing that way.
The entire damned bar wants to meet you
when a Bellini or a Tiziano is sitting there
your fingers around the stem of a glass
like a wilting, wilting rose.
With drinks like these who needs cigarettes.

No such thing as a Canaletto.
Whose name is fluid.

When he was alive
he was known as a greedy-guts chiselling miser
who played on his fame to increase his prices.
He was prolific, thought to be quite well-off.
But when he died there weren't great packets of money
his furniture assessed as junk
the clothes in his closet musty and shabby.
Cloaks in ill-repair, that sort of thing.

On his bargain basement deathbed
did he regret
not having sipped enough of the bubbly?

The problem for bartenders isn't Canaletto's taxable income,
net worth, possible meandering, or ineptitude
with the cold hard cash.
It's the colour.

What do you mix with champagne
to get that
stagnant shimmery steel-blue, gloopy dust-green?
Simply too multifaceted, protean.

Poem Spoiling the Ending of Hemingway's *Across The River and Into the Trees*

He dies, my colonel dies.

He dies a thousand times
but in the end
it's heart
failure.

Failure which is worse than plain death
and indecorous.
But courageous, too.

It's a good ending.
No self-directed gunfire, no sad gondola chase
and he doesn't get the girl, real or imagined.

Sure, it's his rough and true heart
more at home in purgatory than paradise.
Silly and dull, implausible and irretrievable.
That amphibious trinket
beating with the violence of milk.
Unembarrassed.
It folds like so many paper mallards.
Mad shivering organ stinking of rot and decay.

If you have never been in love with anyone in a painting
you may laugh beyond prayer
but for my part
silence.

DETAIL OF GIOVANNI BELLINI'S *YOUNG WOMAN WITH A MIRROR*

In a different understanding of time
there are details of paintings
in which one becomes lost for small infinities.
Corridors,
pools.

Try
the mirror
her slipped halo
try
the back of her head, ornament, wrist
spy through your bunched-up fist
catch
the landscape, terrain, the tricky magic of
indirect glance.

A poem is a powder-puff
mirror held up to another larger mirror.

Sometimes a poem is the dark inside
of fingers like a mead-hall
the tiny grey swallow doing its dangerous, invisible ballet.

DETAIL OF ACCESSORY, TITIAN'S *MADONNA AND CHILD WITH SAINTS JOHN THE BAPTIST AND CATHERINE*

In my mind
I hold this virtuosic yellow skein up to my face
wrap it all around
the better to look at things.

Such a diaphanous garment
has cradled babes
brushed against immaculate blue.

At the end of posing
the model leans back, stands
stretches, then unwinds this flimsy accessory
drops it in a trunk of silk sashes and musty brocades.
It works its way to the bottom
over years
and once is mistaken
for angel dust.

Even starfish clouds will abandon sky
summoned to become messenger of detail,
delight trapped in paint
to live in the black mist
stale air.

This paint-cloud seared by the weight of lust
lost in the simple music of golden rain.

Once this cavern cloud was tethered to sky
its particles are now a frail, desperate inscription of love.
If you could fuse eyes to detail, hold vision upwards
it would tell you of inclement beauty, a world
where you find your soul in the fire of rainbows
but drawn by
spill of honeycomb
the eyes enter flesh and lie down and recline.

(The dream of the Room)

– Ursula dreams a room

Its dimensions are as of a dream
painted, painter looking in a mirror
early morning with coffee and dry bread
his wife still in bed
he lovingly smoothes linen from profane to sacred.

– The room dreams

The room contains all the dreams of those who have slept in it.
Dreams around and through them.
Had believed in the extreme nuances of the moon
in the dead song of night
in calm mornings
in the pleasures of silence.
The room
dreams of angel feathers
caressing its nooks and crannies
is thereafter haunted by its inability to
scream.

LOWER RIGHT-HAND CORNER

Not sunlight, moonlight, starlight, firelight
nor electricity
the glow within dreams of dreams.

Poor, poor Juliet dreams herself through dark caves
incandescent
onto water, turning down narrows
flipping pages
of Baedeker's land of dreams
vaporous vacations
out of Shakespeare into Turner's Venice
inviolable
somnolent
onto another balcony with her Nurse
free of the tragedy of words
smudged into the indomitable inconsequence of paint
into the lower right-hand corner
sightseer of dreams
her back turned to it all
she is small and would ignore the sky, the heavens
indifferent
she looks into the blue and mist over bare shoulder.

And inside that dream
another
another
another
until the last dream
which is forever away

collapses.

Then, perchance, death becomes a different word.
All along it has been entirely the wrong one.

IV

GLUTTONY

BUT RILKE

*"I would almost prefer those who bring back from Venice as their
first and most surpassing memory: the fine pork chop they ate . . ."*
– Rainer Maria Rilke, *Diaries of a Young Poet*

The pigs in Venice
have green velvet wings.
Also, turquoise webbed feet.
And glorious lion's manes.
Scales like mermaids.
Their curly tails are pink
like the sky when the sun goes down over
the basilica.

There, the chops
commune
with your tongue, bring
tears
to your eyes.
Applesauce
condimento ridondante.

Who ever can take anything home?

GLUTTONY OF PAPER

Byron made love,
exiled, on a gluttony of paper.
Wore a clear glass mask
affixed by satin ribbon, purple and gold.
Swam through weeds to sea nymphs, clean
to touch their perfumed bodies with
his imagination a green island.
Lord.
How Romantic.

There was the baker's wife
raisin eyes, sugar-sprinkled thighs
warm and comforting.
When discarded
wounded she broke through glass
attempted to carve her name
on the back of
his hand
like pie.
Because she wanted the draper's wife
to think of her
when tossing silk over blinds midday
when sprinkling water on garments
seducing the poet with damp-folds.

Some day it would be the gondolier's wife
her hair the scent of sea salt
timid winds unheard-of
black paint.
Or the glass-blower's wife

her kiss a perfect O
delicate and gaudy
around her ankles the lingering scent of controlled fires.
There'd be the mask-maker's wife
her abdomen the fragrance
of wet paper and secret glues.

Did he trace vast poems
on their cheeks and flawless limbs with albino feathers
terrified of night, alone
and the dread absent sprawl of black ink?

Mere Echoes of Echoes

". . . we had to deal with phantoms and dust, the mere echoes of echoes . . ." – Henry James, *The Aspern Papers*

Such a fancy burden, these
mere echoes.

Worlds in worlds
in which to blunder and retreat.

For example
the garden
smack dab in the middle of the shabby
gilded sea
and shipwrecked there
two witches
the Misses Bordereau.

Pound of flesh
Romeo and Juliana
roses, roses and more roses
by any other name.
Mere echoes.

Would you call Shakespeare, Mister?

Unnamed narrator sends
devious incendiary flowers
to famished women
in order to come by literary treasure –
famous poet's love letters.

One woman sinks
the other floats away
her barge in invisible flames
she vanishes.

Him foiled,
banished.

The garden left untended
bears pink apricots, wild grapes climb rotting trellis.
A peacock roams in long grass, through prickly rose bushes.
Fog descends and lifts.
The fragrance of just so many absurd blooms
travels across the sea.

DARK CHOCOLATE SIGH

Listen to this last
dark chocolate sigh
my delicious exhalation.
Breathe this dried blood perfume
red wine, chocolate
and laugh, harlequin, laugh.

For death is ridiculous in the end
torture has a comic side, too.

The first sigh
caught me unawares
crossing the bridge
from the Doge's Palace to the prison
I was thinking
give me, instead, a dose of the Inquisitor's famous poison
pour the black liquid into my nostrils
hold the purple and gold vial up to the sun
to see if there's enough for the next fellow.
Or fasten me into one of those
notorious delicate
filigree instruments of torture.
Crush my skull
tear out my tongue
deliciously slow.

The second sigh.
My feet in water, rats grinning at the flesh around my knees
leering at the glistening morsels in my eye sockets.

Don't leave me here, I cried out, to starve and be eaten
to grow feckless gills.

Years of practice, towards perfecting the sigh.
Rolling it out through bars onto the slick green water
into air around gondolas carrying new lovers.
Days and nights
learning to become
that expelled breath
slightest, thin noise from low in the throat.
To see the colour of it in the darkness and dank.
To analyze its intricate redolence.

I have just now finished pleading
to be returned to my palatial room in the dungeon
to my life's work, the labyrinthine sigh.
On the polished table before me
monstrous decanter of wine
plate heaped with shards of chocolate.
Finally, the torture to the death
most appropriate for a starving man
whose mossy ankles have been nibbled by rodents.
I feel the sublime sigh building in my stomach.
Yes, I will stay then, and eat and drink.
And eat and drink. Be merry.

His dinners are brought on silver trays
nothing quite the way he likes.

In a castle in Bohemia
the old librarian is foreign, costumed
flirts with candour
falls in love with a distant garden of mirrors
opens books and devours magical words:
philosophy, languish, voluptuous, gorge, happy.

The servants laugh at him
he fusses his hair
eats oysters and drinks champagne and writes
the grand and glorious dream of his life.

He suspects that he has only fooled people
that he would not haunt unmet women.

He only ever desired desire.
Shelved, he dies among books
drowns in a shallow river of ink
dreaming his name will be breathed
with the names of gods
Adonis Apollo Bacchus.

At the end of love Casanova
opens the sluice gate
to a maze of greed.

His Mind a Venetian Map

Cannot ask for forgiveness.
This weak man.
This is not a poem.
Turns a prison wilderness into a well-balanced garden
flowers, fruit trees, vegetables, berries, paths and lanes.
Utilitarian and beautiful, admirable.
He needs become a better man, different man
or
evaporates.

Cannot neglect the body
when reforming
this is not a poem
the mind.
Thirty laps a day around the garden.
This many dried peas in one pocket
each lap one goes in the other pocket.
At night they rest under a single, thin mattress.
To remind him and remind him.
This is not a poem.

At first when he walks perhaps it is Dante's Inferno.
He's the sort of man who can remember entire books.
Then he strikes upon a trip around the world in his mind.
This is not a poem.
Lonely, lost, he escapes, he dreams.
Becomes a traveller.
Reads travelogues, maps, guides, art histories.
Will cover 31,936 kilometres of 40,000 intended.

Early on, he must have come to Venice.
This is not a poem.
His mind a Venetian map.
Or maps. One shellacked over another, another.
Don't cross this bridge, sleep in a gondola on this canal,
not that one. Here, a secret passageway.
This is not really a church, this monument is false.
Close your eyes, open them, close them.
Visit the Doge's Palace, pass by the prisons, the torture chambers.
So many glass chips, stones, can't count them, don't count.
Ignore Murano altogether, the glass-blower's furnaces.

Escape escape escape.
The beauty.
Makes him happy.
His travels make him happy,
a happy obsession.
Somehow I am glad for him.
This different man.
This weak man.
It passes the time
outside time.
It is a horrifying gladness.
This is not a poem
is not is not a poem
about Albert Speer in Spandau.

V

GLASS OF WATER

MASK-MAKER'S DREAM

It is never easy to fall asleep
after you have devised an insanity of faces
carnival of enchanted stone tourists.

I am on the way to a party
yes yes a masquerade.

A mask is not a disguise
but the planned shipwreck of your desire
languishing on the marshland of your façade.

It falls off, my mask does
not quite a masterpiece
into the slush the gelatinous water
paint separates, glue and paper melt
feathers drown, ribbons become swishing eels.
I am not who I meant to be.
I was nearly lovable.

If you don't know yourself in dreams you are lost.

Unmasked, supremely lonely, vertiginous.
A hall of mirrors.
I don't recognize.
And Venice is the magic word I have forgotten.
I am next to fly from a collapsing campanile
after a tiny green bird.
There have been wars, but I know nothing of them.
Clusters of dark grapes fall from my flowing sleeve
like so many silk scarves.

Eating, I become invisible.
While there are cities in which I meant to dwell
and become mysterious and be loved.
But which now fade, all ugliness.
All spurious.

A maker of masks is decently corrupt.

Drunk, hidden again
I arrive at the party and begin stealing jewels
petty
from the gilded necks and wrists
of those more fortunate.
It matters not that I am no
someone.

I learn who I have been every moment.

GONDOLIER'S DREAM

This black vessel writes fluid lies on water
messages of love and death.

They enter my dream my boat
tourists to some essence of romance
and I, I cannot sing my golden and turquoise arias
not this night.
These lovers costumed in their ripe feelings.
Some take the guise of green apples,
others, peeled plums dipped in raw sugar.

So much love in the world.
Decayed love, tepid or hopeful or crazy love.
Tender love, enchanted love, childish love
the love of a moment.
And every lover wants to see two moons
as if there are no more.
And in my dream I show them a liquid moon
and never the others.
Because alone, without song, I cannot take them
so far.

There are always at least two of me
one rippling in the wake
I leave myself behind over and again.

So much love in the world
so many couples in my gondola
the wind comes up, filigreed fog
we are blown to sea

are wrecked
begin to sink
into realms of water
and only myself alone amphibious.
Always I dream this
sinking.
After days glimpsing so many frail shores.
Do they not realize how tempted Fate is
by all those affairs which take place on water
twice seen?

Water records me like an unremembered dream.

MOSAICIST'S DREAM

Devotion to the meaningful disaster of fragments
is to cheat a gentle and magnificent madness.

I descend from scaffold
and crane heavenward
I see that none of the tesserae belong
have ever belonged, been fixable.
Each piece strays from the facts
intent,
pitiable.

To love something broken is a whisper to lonely gods.

And then I notice my palm heaped with ruin
abandoned gold and red
I notice my hands
crying, gravity
I have grown old somehow, unmysteriously.

A mosaic is a dream fumbled
as you push feet into bedroom slippers.

Next, glass drops like baby teeth
like the eyes of failing chimerae
lozenges pelt onto elaborate marble
neighbourhood children arrive to gorge
ribbon-throated
red-breasted stupid birds
in this violent garden.

New dreams lie down beside every old dream
dying is a seeping and smoothing into the spaces between.

In the dream I am told to reassemble
find something coherent
profoundly ornamental
to attend to the modest radiance of broken things,
shattered
imperfect, lonely.
I begin collecting the bright shiny tiles
it is impossible
and harmless as counting stars.

The sun throws us glittering days
asks us to make peace with glowing wounds
the unhealable
the impatient spaces between
what is and is and is.

CARTOGRAPHER'S DREAM

Anyone who has looked up at the heavens
map in hand
has known death and a thousand wretched goodbyes.

At last, they named Venice the perfect city
as if that could save anyone, all of us.
Immediately the city vanishes
my map the only one left in existence.

The one holding the map is the most solitary figure
standing on the smallest ground.

Plans are announced to rebuild
with strict attention to my map.
I am found out.
You see, I'd never set foot there.
And as they build I try to run away
but it is always towards
this misshapen, half-built,
jewel-laden, dragon-cum-lapdog of a city
from which there is no escape.
I had meant it to be beautiful and breathtaking true
but it lazes slant on the horizon, sluggish, lame, yapping.

Every dream comes with a burning map
a glass of water.

GLASS-BLOWER'S DREAM

Empty.

For days I have been reaching for
this meditative whirling.
I am close to the perfect vessel
the inexpressible stomach
origins.

I gave up words for breath
but then someone was calling for me
calling.

I am full of the blue-orange breath of the universe
fragile igneous calm

a bee
hangs
on my lip
stings.
I cannot move through
this fog of honeybees
lose myself in the hum.

Will you forget to wonder
about everything pushed aside
everything beyond mere surfaces?

Awake, I resume my dream of beautiful failure.

Empty.

ACKNOWLEDGEMENTS

Poems from this collection have appeared in the following jour-nals: *The Canadian Forum, Dandelion, Event,* and *The Fiddlehead*.

This book was written with the support of grants from the Alberta Foundation for the Arts and the Canada Council.

I would like to thank several people for their careful reading and support of my work: Bert Almon, Olga Costopoulos, Meli Costopoulos, Lee Elliott, Michael McCarthy, Iman Mersal, April Miller, Karen Press, and Annette Schouten Woudstra. Thank you to Tim Lilburn, my editor.

Thanks to all my family and Rob's family.

*

The epigraph on page 32 is from *The Stream of Life* by Clarice Lispector (Minneapolis: University of Minnesota Press). Copyright © 1989. Reprinted by permission of the publisher.

The epigraph on page 37 is from *Effie In Venice: Mrs. John Ruskin's Letters Home 1849-52* by Effie Ruskin, edited by Mary Lutyens (London: Pallas Athene). Copyright © 2000. Reprinted by per-mission of the publisher.